MY HAPPY CORNER WITH GOD: IN JESUS' NAME

My Happy Corner with God: In Jesus' Name

Devotionals to Experience the Presence of God

DIANA M YOUNG

7 Tulips Publishing, LLC

Copyright © 2023 by Diana M. Young All rights reserved.

Published by 7 Tulips Publishing, LLC, Tucson, Arizona

Written permission must be secured from the publisher to use or reproduce any part of this book, except for brief quotations in reviews or articles.

Bible versions used in this book are as follows:

Scripture quotations taken from the New American Standard Bible® (NASB), Copyright © 1960, 1962, 1963, 1968, 1971, 1972, 1973, 1975, 1977, 1995 by The Lockman Foundation. Used by permission. www.Lockman.org

Scripture taken from the Holy Bible, NEW INTERNATIONAL VERSION®, NIV® Copyright © 1973, 1978, 1984, 2011 by Biblica, Inc.® Used by permission. All rights reserved worldwide.

Scripture quotations from The Authorized (King James) Version. Rights in the Authorized Version in the United Kingdom are vested in the Crown. Reproduced by permission of the Crown's patentee, Cambridge University Press.

Scripture quotations are taken from the Holy Bible, New Living Translation, copyright ©1996, 2004, 2007, 2013, 2015 by Tyndale House Foundation. Used by permission of Tyndale House Publishers, Inc., Carol Stream, Illinois 60188. All rights reserved.

Scripture quoted by permission. Quotations designated (NET) are from the NET Bible® copyright ©1996-2016 by Biblical Studies Press, L.L.C. http://netbi- ble.org All rights reserved.

The American Standard Version (ASV) is rooted in the work that was done with the Revised Version (RV) (a late 19th-century British revision of the King James Version of 1611). This Bible is in the public domain in the United States.

The Revised Version (RV) or English Revised Version (ERV) of the Bible is a late nineteenth-century British revision of the King James Version. This Bible is in the public domain in the United States.

Library of Congress Cataloging-in-Publication Data is Available:

ISBN 9781733032964 (Paperback)

ISBN 9781733032971 (ePDF)

Cover Design: 7 Tulips Publishing, LLC

Contents

Acknowledgements ix
Introduction x

1	God Challenges Us to Stick to the Plan	1
2	Do You Know Your Purpose, Plan and Destiny?	4
3	Peace	6
4	I am Living a New-Found Life in Jesus' Name	9
5	Going Out into God's Vineyard	12
6	Harvest	14
7	Waiting on the Lord	16
8	Creation	18
9	Blow the Trumpet, Sound the Alarm	21
10	Suffering Trials and Testing	22
11	Entering into the Rest of God	24
12	The Fall	25

13	Blessings in Jesus Name	27
14	Affirmations/Declarations	30
15	Prayers	31
16	Opening Up with Praise and Worship	32
17	Seeking the Lord	35
18	God is Effectively Working in Me. What is He Doing in Your Life?	36
19	Praise Ye the Lord	38
20	You are Kingdom	40
21	Abba Father	42
22	Being Challenged in My Walk	47
23	Glory, Glory, Glory to His Name	50
24	Victory, Victory, Victory in Jesus – Yeshua	52
25	Welcoming the Presence of God: Living, Thriving, Excelling in His Presence	53
26	Jeremiah 1-10	55
27	My Happy Corner with God: In Jesus' Name - Closing Thoughts	57

Acknowledgements

Looking for true loves, and I have found them.

To my spiritual daughter, it is true, God gives you another family. You have been a trooper, helping me in many ways. I thank God for your very life and being.

To my deceased Dad, who was and still is my best friend! To my mom, who did her best in my later years. I have grown to love her so much.

To my sibling and all different personalities, I grew up with; I love you guys.

Introduction

A group of women and I attended a powerful women's retreat. Two dynamic women of God, called, anointed, and appointed, poured out from their hearts. They shared dynamic teaching and preaching. You knew without a shadow of doubt that they had been with the Master. When I returned home from the retreat, I possessed a new zest and zeal for God's Word.

I immersed myself with studying and Bible reading. I ate the Word of God almost 24/7. Reading, writing, and studying were more important to me like ever before.

"But seek ye first the Kingdom of God and his righteousness; and all these things share be added unto you." (Matthew 6:33). This scripture has taken on a whole new meaning for me. My purpose and plan have a brand-new meaning and new direction.

My determination, expectations, and focus have propelled me to a new level of faith, trust and belief in God's Word. God is preparing me to go forth and to do. "Go ye therefore, and teach all nations, baptizing them in the name of the Father, and the Son, and of the Holy Ghost." (Matthew 28:19).

Teaching them to observe all things whatsoever I have commended you: and lo, I am with you always; even unto the end of the world" (King James Version, Matthew 28: 19-20). Amen.

This book is designed to challenge and change your life through the reading of the Word of God and by putting in into action. In this book, you will find life lessons, personal revelations, and God's interventions.

This book is filled with testimonies after testimonies. I have given many examples and proofs that God's Word is true. That you can back everything I have written with God's uncompromising Word.

God's Word will stand forever. Scripture says, in the King James Version, Philippians 1:6, "Being confident of this very thing, that He which hath begun a good work in you will perform it until the day of Jesus Christ".

Chapter 1

God Challenges Us to Stick to the Plan

I have attempted to write books several different times and because of obstacles, hindrances, and many distractions, I stopped. However, this time things will be different. I will not allow anything to stop me. I will listen attentively to the voice of God, and I will obey. People are waiting to read this book.

The world is waiting for the manifestation of the sons of God to manifest themselves. And that includes daughters also.

Manifestation is when something becomes clear or made known.

When we prepare ourselves to be used for the glory of God then manifestation will come. When manifestation comes, the world

will be able to see that we are the sons of God.

(Galatians 4:6-7) 6. And because ye are sons, God hath sent the spirit of his son crying Abba Father. 7. Wherefore though art 90 more a servant, but a son; and if a son, then an heir of God through Christ.

We must make a stand and say what thus saith the Lord. The world is looking for some good news. The Bible is filled with good news. We need to read, trust, and take a stand, because all things, even the bad things, will work together for our good.

King James Version Romans 8:28, "And we know that all things work together for good to them that love God, to them that are the called according to his purpose."

We need to be studying God's word so we will know how to live on planet Earth and go forth. "In the power of God", the Sonship of the Messiah, Jesus Christ, and the sweet Holy Spirit. The holy Spirit is the leader and guider into all truth. We need to be witnessing to the lost and whoever wants to hear about our God, and how Jesus came to redeem us back from the curse of the law.

Chapter 2

Do You Know Your Purpose, Plan and Destiny?

Purpose, plan, and destiny are tied together. Whatever your purpose is, you will develop a passion for it, and you will not allow anything to hinder or interfere. The Lord is helping me fine tune some things that concern my purpose and plan. Once you know God's purpose and plan, your life will take on a new avenue, a new direction. Being in God's perfect will is a great advantage, a guideline that will enable and assist you to continue on.

Then you can decide within yourself to stay the course, no matter what happens. God will be there for you. He will make sure you have the necessary tools to complete your assignment. He and His Word are one. He will never fail you nor leave you; He will add people to you with like precious faith. Scriptures will give you grace and confidence in the God we serve.

Whatever your passion is, usually that is your purpose. However, in the beginning of life's journey you don't know it. As you continue in life's journey, you will find yourself moving towards your purpose and plan. I will speak about me. For some reason, I always liked or had an idea that I would be a teacher. Several years ago, God presented me with that opportunity, and I enjoyed it for a period of time. Now, I am attending a church, and here I am an assistant Sunday school teacher. I am still around children. I must admit this setting and in this season, I just love it.

I enjoy seeing the children's eyes light up, especially when we do projects, and they really get involved: singing, clapping their hands, reciting songs or scriptures. It just blesses me. I am able to give to the next generation, Jesus the Son of the Living God.

Chapter 3

Peace

I was talking to someone the other day, and I was telling them that I had found peace, and I was doing great in the things of God. I proceeded to give a praise report, and the other person kept trying to stop me during the conversation to say there are some things we want to experience for ourselves.

Then I remembered something very profound that my Father said, "Why do you want to experience it, and it is wrong?" I told the person, if someone had told me earlier in life about Jesus and His great love for me, how He died on the Cross for me and my sins, past, present, and future, I could have avoided a lot of disappointments, pain, etc. Right in the midst of my talking, the Holy Spirit began speaking to me: "God's purpose and plan is still being revealed, unfolding in the midst of everything you're going through."

Some things in life we will experience because of inheritance, our up-bringing, the environment in which we live. Because of these different factors, we become a byproduct of our present state of being. We will always go through life's lessons. We learn along the way; and whatever we don't learn, we will repeat, When the time is right, according to God's purpose and plan; He will reveal Himself to us through His Son, Jesus Christ.

Then and only then, will we hear the message, the call, the sermon in whatever vessel God chooses to use. Then we can choose to serve Him or continue in a corrupt, lawless society, living to the dictates of the world and our flesh. Our spirit and our flesh are at enmity with God. We must read the Word of God and acknowledge Jesus Christ as our Lord and Savior.

Romans 10:9-10 says "That if you confess with your mouth the Lord Jesus and believe in your heart that God has raised Him from the dead, you will be saved. For with the heart one believes unto righteousness, and with the mouth confession is made unto salvation."

We must accept, adopt, meditate, and do what God's Word says. When this happens, you'll know you are on your way, on a brand-new journey, a journey you have never experienced.

Life becomes worth living; you change lanes, and you will begin to experience your purpose, plan, and destiny. God's Word will begin to unfold before you.

You will begin to ask yourself questions: "Why am I here? What stance do I need to take next?" You are created on purpose, for purpose, with purpose, and much more.

Chapter 4

I am Living a New-Found Life in Jesus' Name

I recently heard a minister say, "Because of Jesus and what He went through, we have another chance." God sees us through Jesus. Everything He went through, we can or will go through. He has proven everything, from the Cross to the grave, to the sky.

God is omnipotent, omnipresent; he knows all things, and he has many attributes. He is a multifaceted God. He is everything, and he holds everything in the palm of his hands.

Even when we fail, it is no surprise to Him, He's God;

He is always there to help us, no matter what. We are in a 'win-win' situation, as long as we continue to abide in Him, and stay in His Word. God will never leave you nor forsake you, nor fail you; you are never alone.

I heard another minister say, "Jesus did it all." All we have to do is follow the Bible, the Manual, and The Road Map of Life. What we need to do is activate our faith, read, and study God's Word. Build ourselves up on His most Holy faith. When we do that, we build our faith up and our capacity to grow spiritually. Then the world will see we are about our Father's business; Enhancing the Kingdom of God, for "We are the sons of God". (Galatians 4:6-7, Romans 8:14-16 KJV)

Our trust and belief system will open doors no man can close and close doors no man can open. When we walk through this path and continue on it, we will see and experience the miraculous.

New King James Version II Corinthians 5:7 says, "For we walk by faith and not by sight." When we walk through this path and continue on it, we will see and experience the miraculous. No demon no spirit, no man can stop us, or hinder our walk with the Lord.

My goal is to be one of the best soul winners that I can be. Secondly, to be a bestselling author, writing Christian books that will lift up, exhort, and encourage people, telling them they can be everything that God's Word says about them. We are overcomers, winners in every aspect in our lives.

Chapter 5

Going Out into God's Vineyard

The Lord said to me by His Spirit, that He has a new horizon for me as I continue to plow. In the natural plow means to dig up the earth for sowing seed. Spiritually speaking, when we go out and share the gospel of Jesus Christ, we are sowing the Word of God into someone's life/heart.

When we sow good seeds, we will reap a good harvest, a bountiful harvest of good fruit and seeds sharing the good news. We need to always be prepared and ready to share the Gospel of Jesus Christ. Jesus saves, heals, delivers and much more. Jesus is truly the answer to all our problems.

Going out into, God's vineyard, vineyard meaning, plantation of grape vines. We need to be working in God's vineyard, seeking out the lost, cultivating the soil of man's heart with God's Word, watering and giving it nutrients, believing God for the manifestation of good fruit. God's heart and desire for us is to bear "good fruit". We must sow good seeds into our hearts, good wholesome conversation, good deeds, helping others and being there for one another.

Chapter 6

Harvest

We need to bear one another's burdens. When you see someone who has a need, and you have the means, you should help. We need to be there to strengthen one another. We are believing God for a bountiful harvest, a harvest that stands against the contrary winds of life, a weighty heavy harvest of souls that will gladly and joyfully welcome in the Kingdom of God and all His attributes. For the Kingdom of God has come, it has risen because it is within us. Some are ready, and some have yet to get ready.

Then, there are those who don't have a clue of what's going one

Nonetheless, harvest time is coming, we are waiting for the Master with great expectations. Let him who has ears to hear, hear what the Spirit is saying. Wait and listen to the voice of the

Good Shepherd. "I am the good shepherd: the good shepherd giveth his life for the sheep." (New King James Version, John 10: 11).

He is getting ready to come back for us; no one knows the time, nor the hour. Nonetheless, we must get ready and be prepared. For He is truly on His way back for us and what belongs to Him. God made us a promise, and He will not break it. Scripture says, "For all the promises of God in Him, are yes and in Him Amen, to the glory of God through us." (New King James Version, 2 Corinthians 1:20). To God Be the Glory!

Chapter 7

Waiting on the Lord

I was trying to encourage someone who is very dear to me not to be discouraged but learn how to wait on the Lord. The Lord does not like murmuring and complaining. When we continue to practice these behaviors, you are really not trusting God. We cannot bring anything to pass.

We need to do what the Scripture says, relax, and give it to God, because He careth for us. Worrying will do nothing but cause you to become upset and frustrated. It doesn't change the circumstance or the situation and ultimately, it will make you sick and cause health problems. "Ask and it will be given to you; seek and you will find; knock and the door will be opened to you. For everyone who asks receives; the one who seeks finds; and to the one who knocks, the door will be opened" (New International Version, Matthew 7:7-8)

Chapter 8

Creation

During the time of creation, man was in the Father's loins, just like God created and prepared a body for Jesus, Mary. A body was prepared for us. God allowed our parents to get together to bring us forth. It may not have been done properly, but we allowed it, and God by his Spirit moved. Your assignment was ready to be fulfilled, making you the next generation.

Generation is living beings, constituting a single step in a line of descendant production. "But you are a chosen generation, a royal priesthood, a holy nation, His own special people, that you may proclaim the praises of Him who called you out of darkness into His marvelous light." (New King James Version, 1 Peter 2:9)

"This is the book of the genealogy of Adam. In the day that God created man, He made Him in likeness of God." (New King James Version, Genesis 5: 1)

In due time our assignment was ready for us to do what we were called to do. God is the Creator; He created man and formed him from the dust of the earth.

"And the Lord God formed man of the dust of the ground and breathed into his nostrils the breath of life; and man became a living being." (New King James Version, Genesis 2: 7) God is the Creator; He created man with a soul. Your soul consists of your mind, will, and emotions.

Once we arrive and go through life, the necessary process, we will reach our goals and our purpose, being changed from glory to glory, strength to strength, praising our Jesus all the way. I must stop here and give Him glory.

Heaven is God's spiritual home. He created earth for man. "So, God created man in His own image; in the image of God He created him, male and female He created them. Then God blessed them, and God said to them, 'Be fruitful and multiply; fill the earth and subdue it; have dominion over the fish of the sea, over the birds of the air, and over every living thing that moves on the earth'" (New King James Version, Genesis 1:27-28).

Chapter 9

Blow the Trumpet, Sound the Alarm

The past few days have been orchestrated by the Spirit of God. God is a powerful God, invoking His Word, and His Word alone stands firm forever. Who can stand or challenge God's Word?

Who can stand up against it? NO ONE! God is the blesser and the giver of all life. "For God so loved the world, that He gave His only begotten Son, that whosoever believeth in him, should not perish but have everlasting life" (King James Version, John 3: 16).

Chapter 10

Suffering Trials and Testing

The Word of God says in this life we will go through trials, tribulation and testing. Scripture says in King James Version, I Peter 4: 12, "Beloved think it not strange concerning the fiery trial, which is to try you, as though some strange thing happened unto you."

Scripture says in King James Version, John 16:33, "These things I have spoken unto you that in me you may have peace, In the world ye shall have tribulation: but be of good cheer; I have overcome the world." He overcame and so can we; being taught the Word of God is vitally important. The Word of God teaches you how to handle every situation that will come your way. We can, overcome anything by the Blood of The Lamb, and the Word of our testimony.

No one likes going through these obstacles, situations of life; however, we must, and going through these times will show us where we are spiritually. Afterwards, what we have been through can now be a testimony. We will be able to help someone else. If you have never been through anything, how can you help someone else with what they are facing? People, who are hurting, need to hear someone who has made it through, with VICTORY! This is the purpose of your trials and tribulation; it becomes your testimony to help others heal and finish in their own victory through God. "If God can do that for you, He can surely do that for me

But, oh the joy we experience after we have made it over! I like to exhort and encourage people. God's word says once you have been strengthened and delivered, go help your brother and your sister. Who can deny your testimony? That's between you and God; that's your personal conviction.

Chapter 11

Entering into the Rest of God

There is a rest for the people of God who have labored and did what God told them. We are supposed to find rest in the earth. Rest does not mean sit down and do nothing, but to continue and be about the Father's business with ease, not to be troubled or overwhelmed. "So I swear in my wrath, They shall not enter into my rest.)

Take heed, brethren, lest there be in any of you an evil heart of unbelief, in departing from the living God. So, we see that they could not enter in because of unbelief." (King James Version, Hebrews 3:11-12, 19).

Chapter 12

The Fall

Because of the fall, God had to intervene and set up some new rules and regulations. Adam, who had authority, control, and dominion, lost it all to an outlaw spirit, Satan. Now Satan has authority and some control. He is still limited, because God still has ALL POWER is in His hands. Once man starts reading God's Word, the Bible, he can find his way back. Jesus Christ is the Way, the Truth, and the Light. We are created to praise, adore, and magnify the Lord. Everything that God created in the book of Genesis, He said was good. God's Word will continue; His word will be forever.

If only we could listen to the leading and prompting of the Holy Spirit, we would experience a better, wholesome life, rich in abundant blessings. I believe whatever our lot in life is we can turn it around and make it a testimony, a witness to someone, how God can change your life.

We all come and live in the world system, with all our faults and shortcomings. God is no respecter of a person. What He will do for one, He will do for another. God has much work for us to do. All we have to do is prioritize our time, sit down, listen, and get busy.

Chapter 13

Blessings in Jesus Name

Praise Ye the Lord! The Lord showed me, this is a new beginning in my life. I am being changed from glory to glory. I must keep moving. You are walking in that greatness that I have ordained just for you, my daughter. Your resources are here, just continue to ask; When you ask, it will be manifested right before your eyes. I want you to continue and settle down, and just write. Even your journaling, use them as your writing material; for I am speaking to you.

Sometimes prophetically – therefore write it down. Sometimes I share through signs, wonders, visions, and dreams. This is the end times. What does the Word say in the book of Joel? Blow the trumpet in

Zion; let all the inhabitants of the land tremble, for the day of the judgment of the Lord is coming. It is close at hand.

And the Lord shall utter His voice before His army, for His camp is very great; for His is strong and executes His Word, for the day of the Lord is great and very terrible, and who can abide it?

I would like to encourage you, whoever is reading this book, to do a survey within yourself, your scope of wisdom, knowledge, and understanding, what do you want to invest in? Whom do you want to invest in? We need to strive for more. You might say to yourself, I don't want much. Guess what? You won't get much. There's power in your mouth, your tongue. You can speak life or death, blessings, or cursing. I choose to speak life. What about you? Jesus came so that we might have life and have it more abundantly (John 10:10).

In completion of my first book, I thank God for being the Head of my life. Through the years, there have been highs and some lows; however, in the past two years I have seen and experienced God's blessings and much more, He told me in His Word: "There is more to come, because of your faithfulness and obedience to me. I am about to give and fulfill all your promises

Love you daughter, says God".

Chapter 14

Affirmations/ Declarations

Praise will continually be in my mouth. I have made up in my mind, spirit, soul, and body, that I was created for this purpose. To give God unadulterated praise and worship.

Our God is so great! Our God is a Good God, and He will never fail us.

Every time I look around, the Lord keeps blessing me over and over again. God always takes care of what belongs to Him. We are His children, and He is a gentle, caring Father.

Chapter 15

Prayers

"Father God, I thank and praise You, for You are worthy to be praised, Thank You for a perfect peaceful night's sleep, keeping me during the night and waking me up this morning to see a brand-new day filled with your beautiful handiwork."

Now, saith the Lord, turn ye even to Me with all your heart, and with fasting and with weeping and with mourning; and rend your heart, and your garments, and turn unto the Lord your God; for He is gracious and merciful, slow to anger, and of great kindness, and repenteth him of the evil.

Chapter 16

Opening Up with Praise and Worship

Our God is an awesome God

He deserves all the Praise

He deserves all the Glory

He deserves all the Honor

We are created for His purpose just as Jesus, the Son of God sought His Father early in the morning.

Jesus is our example

Jesus is our model

Jesus is our soon-coming King

God gave Jesus a mandate: Ransom back my sons and daughters. Redeem them back from the enemy.

These are my sons and daughters; I created the heavens and the earth.

The heavens are God's habitat, God's dwelling place, the angels' dwelling place.

God created the earth for his sons and daughters.

After God created everything about creation, He said it was and still is good.

Then God wanted a family and side of Himself. That is why even during the time of creation, we know about everything. Because we were in God's loins from the beginning of time.

I believe this is how we can say in our imagination. I have seen this before – believe you did spiritually speaking, you have.

Unless a lot, somethings you are able to remember, and something are like a vision or a dream.

Alleluia, Alleluia Alleluia

Glory to God

Chapter 17

Seeking the Lord

There is a scripture in the Open Bible, it says, "seek the Lord whereby He shall and will be found".

In the Open Bible in Jeremiah 29:13 - 14 "And ye shall seek me and find me when ye shall search for me with all your heart".

And I will be found of you, saith the Lord, and I will turn away your captivity, and I will gather you from all the nations...

Chapter 18

God is Effectively Working in Me. What is He Doing in Your Life?

I give my God all the praise, glory, and honor. I have searched all over and I have found no body greater than Him. I praise and bless His Holy Name.

Writing my second book has brought along with it a different excitement of peace, joy, and happiness and long suffering. It took me approximately 5-7 years to complete my first book. Yes, there were many obstacles, however in my heart, I had already purposed and determined that I was not going to quit. No matter who left me, no matter what sickness, disease and infirmities were attacking my body.

Thinking about what transpired just a year ago. I remember there was a time; when I was going through some dental procedures; not just having 1 tooth extracted, but 2 during the same setting. The next day, I looked into the mirror, and I almost frightened myself! My face looked like I was in a boxing match. The look remained on my face for 3-4 days and talk about pain, my mouth was so sensitive for the next couple of days, I felt like I was having the procedure done over and over again.

Thank you, Father, for your healing virtue, your healing power.

In Jesus' Name.

Chapter 19

Praise Ye the Lord

It is the Father's desire to give you the Kingdom.

FEAR – False Evidence Appearing Real

To God be the glory, for the great things He has in store for us.

Father, I repent and ask for forgiveness for the things I have done.

Today is the day of salvation. Today, I look on forgetting those things which are behind me.

I move forward. I press forward to the high calling in my life. The high calling in the things of God.

I'm not looking back. I'm pressing forward.

For in you all things are forward. I'm moving forward.

Chapter 20

You are Kingdom

And when he was demanded of the Pharisees, when the kingdom of God should come, he answered them and said, The kingdom of God cometh not with observation: Neither shall they say, Lo here! or, lo there! for, behold, the kingdom of God is within you. - Luke 17: 20 – 21

Matthew 6:33 says, But seek ye first the kingdom of God, and his righteousness; and all these things shall be added unto you.

Jesus tells us in this scripture, He teaches that we should not be consumed with external pursuits that are temporary.

But with intercession, our main theme and pursuit is to find the Kingdom of God.

The Kingdom of God is within us.

We need to unpack ourselves and go after the treasure that is within us. Jesus declares, once I locate the Kingdom of God, all these things will be added unto me.

Discovering the Kingdom of God within me will release a level of attraction that I have never experienced.

I will see the resources needed to fulfill the call and purpose of my life. I come to the reality that I need the Trinity.

Chapter 21

Abba Father

Thank you for a super day in and with you.

Today, I was able to take care of some personal things.

It really pays to get up early and seek the Lord.

It really pays to seek the Lord early in the morning.

It seems like after you spend time in His presence, and getting your orders from Him, your days seems to go by a little smoother.

Especially if you have to go out your front door. You don't know who you are going to meet up with, until you meet them.

Our God always—always, has a plan and a purpose for whomever and whatever we are about to encounter.

The Holiday season is upon us. People in the world need to hear some good news. Some need words of encouragement.

They need to know our God. God of the universe – The Creator. God can do anything for them but fail.

The gospel is the good news. The only people who won't accept the good new are those who are walking in darkness and who are denying the power of God.

To believe in a God they can't see, however they can read the manual – the road map – the Bible. It speaks about the attributes of God.

The Creator – the Great I AM. Scripture says come together and let's reason with the Word of God.

How good it is for Brothers to join together in unity.

Then we have the Love chapter. We all can learn a lesson from John 3:16 "For God so loved the world...

We should act like our Beloved Heavenly Father.

What the world needs, what we need is love, genuine love coming from your heart – from the Father's heart to yours.

We need to be there for one another in the unity of the faith, trust and belief.

I should be able to talk and minister to my brothers and my sisters. We need each other.

We need to learn how to bind ourselves with people

with precious like faith and pray earnestly for those who aren't there yet.

Finally, things have begun to line up with and in God's Word.

We have the victory, because we are believers.

Our faith was tried in the fire, and we have come out like pure gold.

Alleluia – God Almighty is a good, good God and Father, He Knows.

I must repeat that again, He knows how to keep and care for those who and what belongs to Him.

Out God is a Keeper – if you're really truly want to be kept.

He will keep you. I don't care what the devil is throwing at you.

I don't care what situation or circumstances plan to entangle you.

God will honor and keep His Word. God only speaks faith-filled words.

Alleluia to the lamb of God. This is what the gospel is about.

Chapter 22

Being Challenged in My Walk

God's Words, says in Proverbs 4:5-9, "Get wisdom, get understanding: forget it not; neither decline from the words of my mouth. Forsake her not, and she shall preserve thee: love her, and she shall keep thee. Wisdom is the principal thing; therefore, get wisdom: and with all thy getting get understanding. Exalt her, and she shall promote thee: she shall bring thee to honor, when thou dost embrace her. She shall give to thine head an ornament of grace: a crown of glory shall she deliver to thee".

The scripture, John 16:13 also says, However, when He, the Spirit of truth, has come, He will guide you into all truth; for He will not speak on His own authority, but whatever He hears He will speak; and He will tell you things to come.

These key verses go hand in hand. They connect and cultivate. They will bring you a weighty, heavy harvest – a good fruit harvest.

You might say what kind of Harvest? We, the Christian- sows, spiritual seeds and we will reap a spiritual harvest for the Kingdom. Whatever you are sowing into the Kingdom of God – that is what we will reap. Present it with your whole heart -- spirit, soul, and body.

God gives seed to the sower. We are supposed to be planning seeds that will bring about a good harvest.

A harvest that will help this generation and the next generation.

Scripture says in the King James Version that whatsoever a man soweth, that he will also reap. In order to reap a good harvest, we must be sowing good seed.

We should be about sowing and cultivating good fruit. I will give you an example. Scripture says in the King James Version He who wins souls is wise. My desire is to be one of the best soul winners, that I can be, In Jesus' Name.

Chapter 23

Glory, Glory, Glory to His Name

God – the Trinity is just awesome – 3 in 1

In my spirit, soul, and body are just elated – on how God is working things out for me, Alleluia, Glory to God.

I recognize that this is my season to experience the favor, the grace, the goodness, and the mercy of God.

I have been speaking, talking, and fellowshipping with the Lord for many years.

Scripture says Philippians 1:6 – He who has begun a good work in thee will complete it until the day of Christ Jesus.

Chapter 24

Victory, Victory, Victory in Jesus – Yeshua

A prophetic moment: Glory to our Most High God

I have been holding this particular family up before the Lord, In Jesus' Name

God prophetically showed me in my spirit how He was going to deal with this family. No in a shameful way, but a caring, giving way. However, more the less – judgement must begin at the house of God.

As when don't repent and get it together personally, God will bring it out publicly. God is an excellent God and He will have order in his house.

Chapter 25

Welcoming the Presence of God: Living, Thriving, Excelling in His Presence

Abba Father

Thank you, Thank you, Thank you

For your awesome presence

This is the day, that the Lord has made

I will rejoice and be glad in it.

Scripture says in the Old Testament scripture, Oh taste and see that the Lord is good and blessed is the man that trusteth in Him.

O how great is thy God

We serve a great, great, great God and there is no one like Him. Alleluia Glory to God.

Chapter 26

Jeremiah 1-10

Father, we pull down the strong hold of division.

We pull down his economical strategies.

We pull it down.

God told us to pray against it.

God said pray and not faint.

Some people are a blessing; some are not.

Our hope is in Christ Jesus.

The Bible said pray – the early church prayed.

It is power when we are together.

The enemy don't want us to be together in prayer.

In the Spirit we are all together.

The early church were in one place, on one accord, and filled with the Holy Ghost and with power.

God is calling us to come in agreement and speak the word of God with boldness and courage.

We get to press from the inside of us.

It takes boldness to do what is right.

God gave us boldness to speak and do.

He gave us power to be courageous in Him.

We need the Holy Ghost.

We need courage.

Chapter 27

My Happy Corner with God: In Jesus' Name - Closing Thoughts

Father God, I thank you for not leaving me. You have a plan and purpose for everyone's life. Hallelujah, Hallelujah, Hallelujah!

You didn't give up on me. Philippians 1:6 says Being confident of this very thing, that He which hath begun a good work in you will perform it until the day of Jesus Christ.

I believe I am on my journey of completion.

In Jesus' Name